Why you should learn Afrikaans:

Learning Afrikaans can be a rewarding experience for several reasons. First, it is a language with a rich cultural and historical heritage, with unique vocabulary, grammar, and pronunciation that reflect its creole origins. Second, Afrikaans is a widely spoken language in South Africa and is recognized as one of the country's official languages. Knowing Afrikaans can help you communicate with South Africans from all walks of life, and can also be useful for business or travel purposes. Third, learning Afrikaans can provide insights into the complexities of South African history and society, and can help to break down cultural barriers and promote understanding between different groups of people.

Whether you're interested in language, culture, history, or simply expanding your horizons, learning Afrikaans is a worthwhile endeavor that can open up new opportunities and perspectives.

5 fun facts about Afrikaans

1. Originating from Dutch, Afrikaans is a **West Germanic language** spoken mainly in South Africa and Namibia, where it has been recognized as one of the 11 official languages.

2. With an estimated **7 million speakers**, Afrikaans is the third most spoken language in South Africa, and is also used by smaller communities in Botswana, Zambia, and Zimbabwe.

3. Afrikaans grammar and vocabulary are simpler compared to Dutch, featuring a reduced verb conjugation and fewer grammatical cases. This makes it **more accessible and comprehensible for learners.**

4. Influenced by **English, Malay, and Bantu languages,** Afrikaans has a unique development history as it emerged from Dutch settlers in the region.

5. Afrikaans is also spoken by small communities of immigrants in other countries, including Australia, Canada, and the United States.

Content

Daily life:
vocabulary related to activities, routines, and common objects in daily life.

Food and drink:
vocabulary related to different types of food, beverages, and cookingtechniques.

Ek staan elke oggend om ses uur op.

→

I wake up at six o'clock every morning

→

ayk stahn el-kuh oh-khund ohm ses yur ohp

→

Ek hou van pizza en pasta.

I like pizza and pasta.

ayk hoh fahn pee-tsa ehn pah-sta

Ek gaan werk om agt uur soggens.

I go to work at eight o'clock in the morning

ayk gahn verrk ohm ahgt yur saw-khens

Ek drink koffie elke oggend.

I drink coffee every morning

ayk dringkaw-fee el-kuh oh-khund

Ek drink elke oggend koffie.

I drink coffee every morning

ayk drink el-kuh oh-khund kaw-fee

Kan ek asseblief 'n glas water kry?

Can I please have a glass of water?

kahn ayk us-suh-bleef un glahs vah-tuhr kray

Ek eet graag ontbyt voor ek
werk toe gaan.

I like to have breakfast
before going to work.

ayk ayt grah-ahg ohnt-bayt fohr ayk verk
too gahn

Ek is allergies vir neute.

I am allergic to nuts.

ayk iss al-ler-kees fir nay-tuh

Ek gaan gereeld oefen by die gym.

I regularly exercise at the gym.

ayk gahn guh-reelt oh-fuhn bay dee khim

Ek het honger.

I am hungry.

ayk het hong-uh

Ek kyk graag TV in die aand.

I like to watch TV in the evening

ayk kuhk grah-ahg tee-vee in dee ahnt

Ek hou van braaivleis en wors.

I like barbecue and sausage.

ayk hoh fahn bry-flays ehn vors

Ek slaap gewoonlik sewe uur per nag.

I usually sleep for seven hours per night.

ayk slaap guh-woon-lik say-vuh yur pur nahg

Kan ek 'n koppie tee kry?

Can I have a cup of tea?

kahn ayk un koh-pee tee kray

Ek ry met die motor werk toe.

I drive to work with my car.

ayk rai met dee moh-tor verk too

Ek het nie lus vir groente nie.

I don't feel like eating
vegetables.

ayk het nee luhs fir khroon-tuh nee

Ek koop elke week kos by die supermark.

I buy groceries every week at the supermarket.

ayk koop el-kuh week kaws bay dee soo-per-mark

Ek hou van suiker in my koffie.

I like sugar in my coffee.

ayk hoh fahn soo-ker in may kaw-fee

Ek lees 'n boek voor ek gaan slaap.

I read a book before going to sleep.

ayk lays un boohk fohr ayk gahn slaap

Kan ek 'n stukkie sjokolade hê?

Can I have a piece of chocolate?

kahn ayk un stuh-kee shoh-ko-lah-duh hay

Travel:
vocabulary related to transportation, accommodations, and tourism.

Health and medicine:
vocabulary related to illnesses, injuries, treatments, and medical professionals.

Ek gaan met die trein na Kaapstad.

I am taking the train to Cape Town.

ayk gahn met dee treyn na kahp-staht

Ek het 'n hoofpyn.

I have a headache.

ayk het un hohf-payn

Ek wil graag 'n hotelkamer bespreek.

I would like to book a hotel room.

ayk vill khrahgh un hoh-tel-kahm-er buh-spree-k

Ek voel naar.

I feel sick.

ayk foyl naar

Waar is die lughawe?

Where is the airport?

vahr iss dee luuh-gah-weh

Ek moet 'n afspraak maak met die dokter.

I need to make an appointment with the doctor.

ayk moht un af-sprahk maahk met dee dohk-tuhr

Ek huur 'n motor vir die week.

I am renting a car for the
week.

ayk hyur un moh-tuhr fir dee week

Ek het my arm gebreek.

I broke my arm.

ayk het may ahm guh-breyk

Ek gaan op 'n toer na die Krugerwildtuin.

I am going on a tour to Kruger National Park.

ayk gahn ohp un tohr na dee kroo-gher-vihld-toyn

Waar is die apteek?

Where is the pharmacy?

vahr iss dee ap-tayk

Ek is op soek na 'n goeie restaurant.

I am lookingfor a good restaurant.

ayk iss ohp sook na un khoy-duh res-tow-rahnt

Ek moet medikasie neem vir my allergieë.

I need to take medication for my allergies.

ayk moht meh-di-kah-see nuhm fir may al-ler-ghee-uh

Kan ek 'n kaartjie koop?

Can I buy a ticket?

kahn ayk un kahr-tchee koop

Kan ek 'n doktersbriefie kry?

Can I get a doctor's note?

kahn ayk un dohk-tuhrs-bree-fee kray

Ek wil graag 'n vlug bespreek.

I would like to book a flight.

ayk vill khrahgh un fluhkh buh-spree-k

Ek het 'n afspraak met die tandarts.

I have an appointment with the dentist.

ayk het un af-sprahk met dee tund-ahrtss

Waar is die dorpshuis?

Where is the town hall?

vahr iss dee dohrps-hoy-s

Ek het 'n koue.

I have a cold.

ayk het un koh-uh

Ek slaap in 'n jeugherberg.

I am stayi n gin a youth hostel.

ayk slahp in un yoohg-her-berkh

Ek moet na die hospitaal gaan.

I need to go to the hospital.

ayk moht na dee haws-pi-tahl gahn

Education:

vocabulary related to academic subjects, degrees, and educational institutions.

Business:

vocabulary related to finance, marketing management, and entrepreneurship.

Ek studeer ingenieurswese.

I study engineering

ayk stoo-deer in-khay-nyeurs-vay-seh

Ons het 'n plan vir besigheidsgroei.

We have a plan for business growth.

ons het un plahn fir buh-sih-gehts-groh-ee

Ek het 'n graad in rekeningkunde.

I have a degree in accounting

ayk het un grahd in reh-keningkuhn-duh

Wat is jou besigheidsplan?

What is your business plan?

vut iss yoh buh-sih-gehts-plahn

Waar is die universiteit?

Where is the university?

vahr iss dee yoo-nuh-ver-suh-tate

Ek het 'n lening by die bank geneem.

I took out a loan from the bank.

ayk het un lay-ni ng buy dee bungk guh-neem

Ek is 'n eerstejaar student.

I am a first-year student.

ayk iss un ay-stuh-yaahr stoo-dehnt

Ek werk vir 'n groot maatskappy.

I work for a large company.

ayk vuhrk fir un groht maht-skah-pee

Ek doen navorsing in biologie.

I am conducting research in biology.

ayk doo-en nah-fohr-sing in bee-oh-loh-gee

Ons het 'n nuwe bemarkingsplan nodig.

We need a new marketing plan.

ons het un noo-weh buh-mahr-kings-plahn noh-dihk

Ek het 'n beurs gekry.

I received a scholarship.

ayk het un buhrs kuh-ree

Ek is die bestuurder van 'n besigheid.

I am the manager of a business.

ayk iss dee buh-stoo-ur-duhr van un buh-sih-geht

Ek studeer aan 'n kollege.

I study at a college.

ayk stoo-deer ahn un kohl-leh-geh

Ons het 'n beleggingsgeleentheid gevind.

We found an investment opportunity.

ons het un buh-lehg-gi ngs-guh-leynt-hayt guh-find

Ek het 'n skooltoekenning gekry.

I received a school award.

ayk het un skohl-too-kuh-ni ngkuh-ree

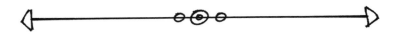

Die aandelemark is baie wispelturig.

The stock market is very volatile.

dee ahn-deh-luh-mahrk iss bay-uh wis-puhl-tuh-rukh

Ek is 'n dosent in geskiedenis.

I am a lecturer in history.

ayk iss un doh-sent in ghuh-skhee-deh-nis

Ek wil 'n besigheid begin.

I want to start a business.

ayk vil un buh-sih-geht bi-tin

Waar kan ek 'n kursus in Afrikaans vind?

Where can I find a course in Afrikaans?

vahr kahn ayk un kur-sus in af-ri-kaans fint

Ons het ons jaarverslag voltooi.

We have completed our annual report.

ons het ons yahr-fehr-slahkh fuhl-toh-ee

Art and culture:
vocabulary related to literature, music, cinema, and visual arts.

Sports and fitness:
vocabulary related to sports, exercises, and fitness equipment.

Hierdie boek is 'n klassieker in die literatuur.

- -

This book is a classic in literature.

heer-dee buh-uhk iss un kluh-see-kuhr in dee lih-tuh-rah-tuhr

Ek hou daarvan om te hardloop in die oggende.

- -

I like to go for a run in the mornings.

ayk ho-uh dah-ruh-vuhn ohm tuh hahrt-lohp in dee oh-kuhn-ghuh

Die orkes het 'n pragtige
vertoninggelewer.

The orchestra gave a
splendid performance.

dee ohr-kuhs het un prahk-tih-kuh vuhr-
toh-ning guh-ley-vuhr

Die span het die kampioenskap
gewen.

The team won the
championship.

dee spahn het dee kum-pee-un-skahp guh-
wen

Hierdie fliek het baie
toekennings gewen.

This movie has won many
awards.

heer-dee flayk het bay-uh too-ken-nings
guh-wen

Hierdie oefening is goed vir jou
buikspiere.

This exercise is good for
your abs.

heer-dee oo-uh-fuh-ning iss goot fuh-r yoh
boyk-spee-ruh

Ek hou van om te skilder in my vrye tyd.

I like to paint in my free time.

ayk ho-uh vun ohm tuh ski-uhl-duhr in may vry-uh tid

Die stoot is 'n gewilde atletiekbyeenkoms.

Shotput is a popular athletics event.

dee stoh-ut iss un guh-wil-duh uh-tluh-tik-bee-yuhn-kohms

Sy is 'n bekende aktrise in die rolprentbedryf.

She is a famous actress in the film industry.

see iss un buh-kuhn-duh uhk-trih-suh in dee rohl-praynt-buh-drihf

Ek gebruik 'n hometrainer om fiks te bly.

I use a stationary bike to stay fit.

ayk ghuh-brayk un hohm-tray-nuhr ohm fiks tuh blay

Die ballet was 'n skouspelagtige vertoning

The ballet was a spectacular performance.

dee buh-lay was un skou-speh-luhk-tih-kuh
vuhr-toh-ning

Hierdie gym het baie toerusting om mee te oefen.

This gym has a lot of equipment to exercise with.

heer-dee ghaym het bay-uh too-ruh-sting
ohm may tuh oo-fuhn

Ek geniet om musiek te maak op my kitaar.

I enjoy makingmusic on my guitar.

ayk guh-nee-uht ohm my-yuk tuh mahk ohp may kih-tahr

Die rugbyspan het 'n harde wedstryd gehad.

The rugby team had a tough game.

dee ruhgh-bee-spahn het un hahr-duh vut-strayd guh-haht

Die skrywer het 'n nuwe boek uitgereik.

The author has released a new book.

dee skray-vuhr het un noo-weh buh-uhk oy-tuh-ryk

Ek hou daarvan om te swem vir oefening

I like to swim for exercise.

ayk ho-uh dah-ruh-vuhn ohm tuh svaym fuhr oo-fuh-ning

Hierdie skildery is geskilder deur 'n beroemde kunstenaar.

This painti ngwas painted by a famous artist.

heer-dee ski-uhl-duh-ree iss guh-skil-duhr dur un buh-roo-muh-duh kuhns-tuh-nahr

Hierdie apparaat help om jou armspiere te versterk.

This machine helps to strengthen your arm muscles.

heer-dee uh-puh-rah-uht help ohm yoh ahrm-spee-ruh tuh fuhr-staynk

Ek het 'n baie interessante dokumentêr gesien.

I watched a very interesting documentary.

ayk het un bay-uh in-tuh-ruh-sahn-tuh duh-koh-mun-tayr guh-see-uhn

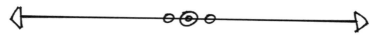

Die atleet het 'n nuwe rekord gebreek.

The athlete broke a new record.

dee uh-tleht het un noo-weh ruh-kohrd guh-breyk

Internet and technology:
vocabulary related to social media platforms, mobile devices, and digital communication.

Relationships:
vocabulary related to family, friends, romantic relationships, and social interactions.

Ek het my vriend op Facebook gevolg.

I followed my friend on Facebook.

ayk het may vriend ohp Fays-boohk ghuh-fuhlg

Ek het 'n groot gesin.

I have a large family.

ayk het un gro-ot guh-sin

Die selfie het baie harte gekry
op Instagram.

- -

The selfie got a lot of
hearts on Instagram.

dee sell-fee het bay-uh hahr-tuh ghuh-kree
ohp In-stuh-grahm

My beste vriendin is baie lojaal.

- -

My best friend is very loyal.

may bes-tuh friend-in iss bay-uh loy-ahl

Ek het 'n nuwe selfoon gekoop.

I bought a new cellphone.

ayk het un noo-weh sell-fohn guh-kohp

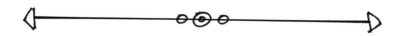

Ek is getroud met my sielsgenoot.

I am married to my soulmate.

ayk iss guh-trowt met may seels-ghuh-noot

Hierdie app is baie nuttig vir reisigers.

This app is very useful for travelers.

heer-dee uh-p iss bay-uh noo-tuhkh fuhr ry-suh-ruhs

Sy is my hartsvriendin.

She is my best friend.

see iss may hahrts-frehn-din

Die video-oproep het goed
gewerk op Skype.

The video call worked well
on Skype.

dee fuh-dee-oh oh-prohp het goot guh-
werk ohp Skaip

Ons het 'n baie goeie
verhoudi ng

We have a very good
relationship.

ohns het bay-uh gwee-uh vuhr-how-di ng

Ek stuur gereeld boodskappe
na my familie op WhatsApp.

I regularly send messages
to my family on WhatsApp.

ayk stoo-uhr guh-reelt boot-skah-puh nuh
may fuh-muh-lee ohp Wots-uh-p

Ek het my boetie lief.

I love my little brother.

ayk het may boo-tie leaf

Hierdie toepassing maak dit maklik om te e-pos.

This application makes it easy to email.

heer-dee toh-puh-sing mahk dit mahk-lik ohm tuh ee-pohs

Ek waardeer ons vriendskap baie.

I value our friendship a lot.

ayk vah-reh-dehr ohns frehnts-kuhp bay-uh

Ek speel graag spelletjies op my tablet.

I enjoy playi n ggames on my tablet.

ayk spay-uhl grah-ahg spel-luh-chuhs ohp may tah-blit

Hy het my gevra om sy meisie te wees.

He asked me to be his girlfriend.

hay het may guh-vrah ohm say may-see-uh tuh vays

Hierdie rekenaar het baie
geheue.

This computer has a lot of
memory.

heer-dee ruh-kuh-nahr het bay-uh guh-hoy-
uh

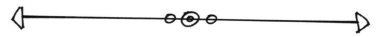

Ons het 'n groot vriendegroep.

We have a large group of
friends.

ohns het gro-ot friend-uh-groop

Die WiFi-verbindi ng is baie stadig.

The WiFi connection is very slow

dee WiFi-vuhr-bin-di ngiss bay-uh stuh-dig

Hierdie persoon is my kollega.

This person is my colleague.

heer-dee pair-sohn iss may kuhl-lay-gah

Vocabulary: Daily Life

1. oggend (morning)

2. uur (hour)

3. werk (work)

4. soggens (in the morning)

5. ontbyt (breakfast)

6. graag (like)

7. gaan (go)

8. gereeld (regularly)

9. oefen (exercise)

10. aand (evening)

11. slaap (sleep)

12. gewoonlik (usually)

13. nag (night)

14. ry (drive)

15. motor (car)

16. koop (buy)

17. kos (groceries)

18. lees (read)

Vocabulary: Travel

1. trein (train)

2. Kaapstad (Cape Town)

3. hotelkamer (hotel room)

4. lughawe (airport)

5. huur (rent)

6. motor (car)

7. toer (tour)

8. kaartjie (ticket)

9. vlug (flight)

10. dorpshuis (town hall)

11. jeugherberg (youth hostel)

Vocabulary: Education

1. studeer (study)

2. ingenieurswese (engineering)

3. graad (degree)

4. rekeningkunde (accounting)

5. universiteit (university)

6. eerstejaar (first-year)

7. navorsing (research)

8. biologie (biology)

9. beurs (scholarship)

10. kollege (college)

11. skooltoekenning (school award)

12. geskiedenis (history)

13. kursus (course)

Vocabulary: Art and Culture

1. boek (book)

2. literatuur (literature)

3. orkes (orchestra)

4. vertoning (performance)

5. fliek (movie)

6. toekennings (awards)

7. skilder (paint)

8. vrye tyd (free time)

9. aktrise (actress)

10. musiek (music)

11. kitaar (guitar)

12. skrywer (author)

13. skildery (painting)

14. kunstenaar (artist)

15. dokumentêr (documentary)

Vocabulary: Food and Drink

1.   pizza (pizza)

2.   pasta (pasta)

3.   asseblief (please)

4.   glas (glass)

5.   water (water)

6.   allergies (allergic)

7.   neute (nuts)

Printed in Great Britain
by Amazon

40153871R10035